MAKING A HOME
FOR FAERIES

BY ROBBIE ADKINS

Published in the USA by:

ADKINS CONSULTING

45981 Classic Way
Temecula, CA 92592
www.voiceofsoul.org

ISBN: 978-1537028170
Printed in the United States of America
Book design by Robbie Adkins, www.adkinsconsult.com
facebook.com/BuildingFaerieHouses
www.voiceofsoul.org
www.adkinsconsult.com

TABLE OF CONTENTS

IV

DEDICATION

THIS BOOK IS DEDICATED to all those grown-ups that still remain open to the magical beliefs of their childhood.

I am also grateful for the editing skills of Linda Bartz, who did a great job of cleaning up my unique writing style, to Marleen Adkins, Nikki Gomez and Robbie Nelson for checking the clarity of my instructions, to Beverlee Harbour Gopp who encouraged me to write this book, to Marilyn Harper who continues to help me connect with my soul purpose, and of course, to my husband, Dale H. Polk.

INTRODUCTION

I HAVE ALWAYS BEEN FASCINATED with the idea of Faeries and Nature Spirits, but admit I have never seen one. I have read books about them, and I do believe they exist, helping care for the plant and animal world, but that we have lost our ability to see them. I also believe that it is time for us to reconnect with them, and to respect their role in fostering life itself. I think it is possible there are some nasty Faeries too, but I am not interested in them.

This book is my story of attempting to reach out and connect with Faeries. As I understand it, they do not generally trust humans, and why should they? Mankind has taken the stance of "controlling" nature by force of will for many, many centuries. I think we can all see that right now that, isn't working out so well for us!

So, gently, I reach out and encourage others to do so. This book is my simple way of doing that. I have built several "Faerie Houses" for inside and outside our home, but believe only one of them is most certainly inhabited. That is the first one I built, and I built it because I noticed the magical health of the orchids in my kitchen window.

I then ventured outside and built two more Faerie Houses that are more sturdy in structure. I can't say that anyone has taken up residence there, but the experience with the pond Faerie House turned into a grand adventure with nature quite different than what I expected.

I have included instructions to build houses like the ones shown here, but I encourage you to create your own dwellings, too. For instance, I don't really know how tall to make the doors! I do believe in keeping the materials as natural as possible, and I always try to include a crystal or "sparkle" of some kind.

So, have fun and venture out! Do this activity with children, as they have not yet shut down to the possibilities that these magical creatures just might exist. Send me photos, and your stories. Perhaps we will make another book, or at least a facebook page, of your creations AND potential encounters with our nature friends.

BEFORE YOU BEGIN ...

Depending on your level of experience, some of the terms, tasks and materials I describe might be confusing to you; so, if something isn't clear, please refer to these pages.

Watercolor paper. I purchase large single sheets that are available at most art supply stores. For these projects, I used Arches watercolor paper, natural white, rough finish, 140 lbs. Any watercolor paper will do as long as it is thick enough, so I wouldn't use less than 140 lb. paper, any finish.

To cut out the pieces, first cut out your patterns, and then tape to the paper. Use a good quality sharp X-acto® knife. For straight edges, I always use a metal ruler on the line to guide the knife. For the parts that you are to score only, poke a hole at both ends of the straight line and, after your piece is cut out and the pattern removed, use either the back (dull) side of the X-acto knife or something like a metal nail file, and using the ruler as a guide, run along that line to 'score' the paper so it will make a crisp clean fold. Practice on some scrap pieces of paper to learn the right amount of pressure to use. Too much pressure and you will cut through the paper – too little, and you won't get a very straight fold.

Clear Matte Acrylic Paint. For this, I purchased Liquitex® Clear Gesso, available at art supply stores. If you don't coat the paper after you are finished with your decorative painting, it will absorb water from the air in the room and change shape. It looks white as it goes on, but dries clear.

Watercolors and brushes. This is not the place to save money! If you use a good quality watercolor paint, your art work will never fade. I have pieces that have been exposed to light for 35 years, and have not faded at all. I prefer to use tubes of watercolor paint and a mixing palette, but solid watercolors work fine, too, as long as they are a good brand. For a very different look, you can also use acrylic paints.

For the brushes, buy a couple different sizes of good quality brushes that come to a fine point. For these small pieces, you really need just a small brush for details, and a larger brush for wash areas. Better to buy two good brushes than a set with sizes you won't even use.

Crystal Beads and Pearls. Because I also make jewelry, I have a ready supply of these, but the very best place I have found to purchase them is Fire Mountain Gems, http://firemountaingems.com/. The pearls are fresh water pearls, come in many sizes and colors, and are not expensive. For the crystal beads, they often come as a strand, and can also be reasonable. They sell Swarovski® crystal beads, but I prefer to use real crystal gemstones.

Twigs. For these, I happen to have some birch trees in my yard, and when the wind blows down little branches, I pick them up and keep them. Even if you live in an urban area, there are always parks or trees around. Just try to find straight pieces. Also, stores like Michaels® have a good supply of stick-like organic things.

Tiles. Tilebar, http://tilebar.com/, will send you samples of tiles, and they have small ones for these kinds of projects. I like them when I want to put in a window of some kind.

Glue. For the most part, I use a hot glue gun; however when I first glued the pine cone scales to the copper foil, after a while, they started to release. The glue remained attached to the copper, but for some reason, let go of the scales. I have also used Gorilla Glue®, which takes a while to set and does expand as it sets. E6000® also works, but is much slower to set.

'Expanding' Gorilla Glue.

Clay. For the clay window and door dressings for the wine cork house, I used Kato Polyclay™, also from Fire Mountain Gems. I used the translucent, and mixed in some iridescent glitter before shaping; however, the clay never dried totally transparent.

Anything else ... If you get stuck with finding something, just email me and I'll see if I can help. The important thing to remember with these projects is that found materials are the best, most natural to use. If you can't find something exactly to your liking, open up your imagination and look for a good substitute! Let the materials direct your creation!

I have described here what I have created, but these are really guidelines to your imagination. Let the Faeries tell YOU what they want their homes made of!

HOW IT BEGAN FOR ME - THE ORCHID FAERIE

I HAVE ALWAYS LOVED ORCHIDS, and when I lived in San Diego, had great success with growing them outside; but when we moved to Temecula, the air was too hot and too dry to support them. I started buying them for inside the house. I was given some orchids, too, and I believe this all started with one that I was gifted.

I had this one plant on the dining room table for a long time, then moved it to the kitchen window. The flowers lasted for 5 months! None of them died or withered, for the longest time. I was amazed, and decided that they were being attended by an Orchid Faerie. I don't know why I thought that, but that is what came to me.

I decided that I should make a little home for the Faerie to live in, next to the orchid plants. I had a few of them by this time. That was the inspiration for my first Faerie House.

I had read enough about likes and dislikes of Faeries that I knew I should use all natural materials. I had a lot of experience working with watercolor paper and paper sculptures, so decided to make the house out of paper, and paint the details on it. I made the "floor" of twigs, and covered it with moss for the comfort of the Faerie. I put a crystal outside the front door, as I understand Faeries like them. I made a thatched roof of lavender from my own yard. I kept the door open, so the Faerie could go in and out, and made a window with shutters that are open to see in and out. I painted an orchid on the far wall for the entertainment of the Faerie.

That was in 2014.

I continued to have good luck with the orchids re-blooming, but I noticed that the plant closest to the Faerie House started growing air roots ... toward the house! Orchids often have roots that are above ground that draw moisture from the air. If you water the roots that are below the plant too much, it won't be happy, and might die. Orchids don't like wet feet. But this was amazing. It hadn't had many air roots, and it started growing them as if to reach out to the house! As I write this in the summer of 2016, the roots seem to want to grow right around the house! To me, this is evidence of the Faerie living there! I have never seen the actual Faerie ... or any Faerie for that matter ... so I am not sure what size they are. But I can FEEL the energy of this one. The closest experience

I have had to "seeing" it is that one day, the paper towel holder on the counter next to the Faerie House started to flutter. There was NO motion in the room – not from me, not from an open window. I just watched it in amazement.

This summer of 2016, the orchids are blooming beautifully again, and the long stems of the orchid plants are all reaching towards the Faerie House! Usually, those stems are staked to be straight up, but I just let them grow where they wanted this year – and they ALL leaned toward the house! The flowers have been there for several weeks now, and show no signs of aging.

ASSEMBLY

You will need:

- heavy watercolor paper
- watercolor paint and brushes
- twigs
- moss
- a crystal
- hot glue and hot glue gun
- clear matte acrylic paint
- roofing material such as lavender
- an X-acto® knife

After you have picked a spot somewhere inside your house were plants seem to do really well, decide what kind of Faerie you want to invite to stay there ... usually one that favors the kind of plant that is doing well in that spot.

Use a heavy weight water color paper, and cut out the sides of the house using the pattern provided here. Cut the door and shutters to open slightly while you are painting them. Decide on your colors and decorations, and enjoy the process of painting the outside and the inside of your house. When it is dry, coat with the clear acrylic to prevent too much moisture absorption.

Next, gather your twigs, and make a square of the twigs that is 3" x 4", and hot glue the corners together (see the photo to the right.) The twigs you use for the outside frame should be thicker than the ones used as crosshatches. Then, lay lighter pieces of twig across that frame and hot glue in place. I left some longer pieces in the center of the front to support the little porch at the front door. After all, as far as we know, the Faeries have no significant weight, so the porch can be a fairly delicate structure.

Do the same thing to make the roof, making two shapes the same size. Then, hot glue the two sides together at the top and make a cross brace that is 3" long at the bottom of both ends. Hot glue the roof together. Then, hot glue your roofing material in layers across the top of the roof frame. I found lavender growing in my yard, and it has held up fine. I didn't want to use a plant that would offend the orchids or the Faerie, but they seem OK with the lavender. You just have to have your own sense about what works together and what doesn't.

When finished, hot glue the house together at the corner, glue to the base frame. Fit your torn piece of paper to make the porch and hot glue in place. Next put your moss in from the top, and make sure it is soft and in all the corners – then glue the roof to the top. To finish, I hot glue the crystal by the front door and glue a loop of twine on the back near the top to hang the house on the wall.

Finally, invite anyone that wants to come live there to please do so, and tell them you appreciate them, and will be happy if they decide to live there. Tell them you mean them no harm!

Viewing from the bottom, there are longer twigs in the center front to support the "porch."

I chose to put wings above the front door.

On the inside wall, I painted an orchid flower for the entertainment of the Faerie.

This side faces the window, so I put some decoration on this side.

I found this nice crystal at a farmers market. Not expensive and very clear.

On the back, at the base of the roof, I hot glued a piece of twine to hang the house from.

In the Spring of 2016, the roots of the closest orchid plant are attracted to the Faerie House. The yellow orchid fell that way, and the purple (yet to bloom) is really reaching its long arm that way, too!

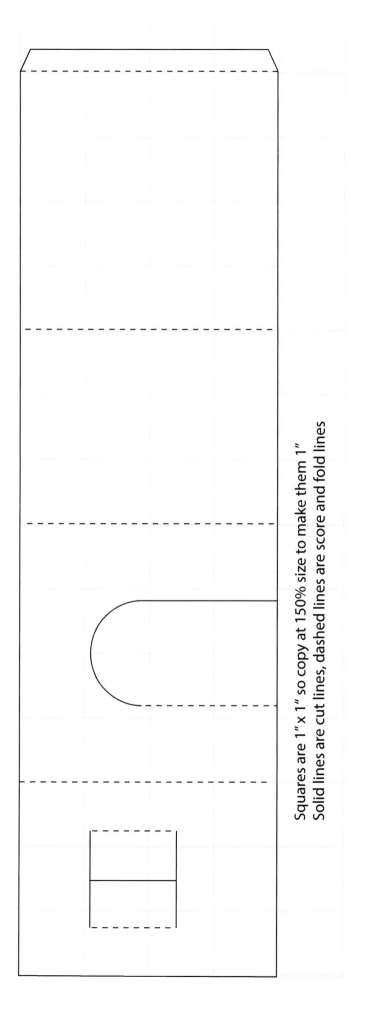

Squares are 1" x 1" so copy at 150% size to make them 1"
Solid lines are cut lines, dashed lines are score and fold lines

Copy this template for the Orchid Faerie House at 150% to get close to the 1" grid.

14

TIME TO MOVE OUTSIDE!

NEXT, I DECIDED that I would make a more sturdy house for a Faerie to live outside. We don't have snow but once every 10 years or so, but we do have constant, heavy winds because of our specific location, and we get below freezing many days during the winter. We are well into the 100's several times in the summer.

I had a lot of wine corks (hmm ... wonder why!), and had a metal shelf outside in the back of the house that was never used. I tried putting things on it, but if it was a plant, I would forget to water it (due to the wind, it would dry out almost every day,) or objects like candles would blow right off onto the ground. The shelf was very near a beautiful wisteria vine I

The wisteria has grown under the sidewalk in the middle of the gardenias and keeps trying to grow up the wall to the Faerie House, no matter how many times I cut it back to the ground!

had planted when we moved here that had grown to great volume, so I decided it was a place for the Wisteria Faerie to live, a little protected from harsh weather conditions.

16

Now, as I am writing this, I am realizing that the wisteria keeps sending branches out of the ground, right next to the Faerie House on the wall. The main vine is on the other side of the sidewalk, and I keep cutting these sprouts down to the base, but THEY KEEP COMING BACK! So, I have to wonder, if they are trying to reach the Wisteria Faerie, just like the orchids are drawn to the Orchid Faerie! Up until now, their insistence at growing where they don't belong has been an irritation ... but now, I believe I understand why!

I have had to make some modifications to this little house along the way. The first roof I made, from some glass tiles I had, was supported by the frame of little twigs ... but the glass was too heavy, especially for the twigs. So then, I replaced that roof with a piece of copper foil, and covered it with 'shingles' clipped from a pine cone. That worked really well, but I used hot glue, and eventually the pieces of pine cone came loose from the hot glue. I thought hot glue would work on anything! So now, I am resorting to Gorilla Glue®!

On a trip to Portland to see family, I got some little decorations from a nursery there. Bicycle? Where would the Faerie ride it? Well, this is for the fantasy of the humans too, isn't it? There is a lantern and a flower pot, too. I also found a card with a beautiful

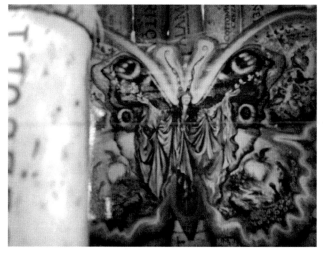

Looking through the front door, you can see the beautiful Faerie art on the back wall.

There are glittery shutters on the windows for a minor amount of privacy!

The 'side yard' has a bench, bicycle, a welcoming Faerie, a potted flower and the lantern.

The other side has a beautiful rock tucked behind and a tree made with moss glued on a twig.

The small twigs were not enough to support the heavy glass tiles ... so I removed the tiles ... the hot glue remained

Then replaced the roof with a piece of copper foil with pine cone scales.

Faerie on it, cut it out, and laminated it so the Faerie would have art to look at. The lamination would protect it from the harsh weather.

The doors and windows are open, but I found some glittery clay that I shaped into shutters and an arch above the front door.

My big issue now is what to do with the wisteria that won't stop trying to invade the Faerie House, and our house as well! As they always say, be careful what you ask for, as you might just get it!

ASSEMBLY

You will need:
• minimum of 88 wine corks   • twigs for floor and roof support   • moss   • a crystal
• knife for cutting corks   • hot glue and hot glue gun   • Gorilla Glue®
• copper foil from craft store   • glitter shapeable clay
• some kind of roofing shingles, such as pine cone scales or sea shells
• If you don't have a metal or wood shelf, then some kind of sturdy base
• decorative elements from nursery or craft store

18

After you have picked a spot somewhere outside near a plant that seems to be doing well, or that you would LIKE to do well, decide if your Faerie House will sit on a shelf or on the ground.

Start by making the sides of your house, by cutting and hot gluing your corks together. Once you have done that, then you can measure to see how big to make your base frame with cross supports and your roof frame, out of twigs. Use bigger twigs for the outside of the frame. Leave some longer twigs to extend out the front door to make a 'porch.'

Glue the floor frame to the base you have decided upon, then hot glue the walls together to make the house itself. Put moss on the floor inside, and add any decorative art work to the inside walls. Shape your window shutters and arch above the front door, and let the clay set. Decorate these with any glittery crystal beads you might have around. When the window shutters and arch have hardened, hot glue them to the cork house.

Cut the copper foil to the right size for the roof, and add the shingles. At first, I used hot glue but the pine cone scales started to detach with time, so had to be repaired with

Gorilla Glue®. When completed, glue to the top of the house. Fill the 'gaps' between the roof and the corks with moss so the house doesn't have a 'whistle' as the wind blows through those narrow spaces.

Now, have some fun with the details you add, inside and out. I made a tree to sit behind the house out of a twig and moss, and added a pretty quartz rock. You can see all the other goodies I added too. We don't know for sure WHAT the Faeries like, so tap into your intuition to see if you can make a good guess.

For the final (hopefully) chapter about the roof of this house, it now has a third version. The hot glue stuck to the copper but the pine cone scales eventually started to fly away in the wind – so I purchased some small shells from the craft store, and this time used Gorilla glue. You might want to start with this plan in the first place!

Organizing the sea shells.

The third and hopefully final roof for the wine cork Wisteria Faerie House!

Patterns for the four walls of the wine cork Wisteria Faerie House. These drawings are not to scale but represent using standard wine corks.

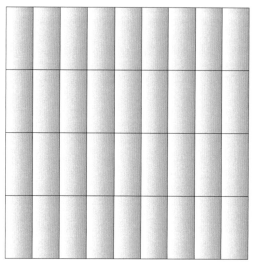

Cork pattern/back wall

I made the back wall 9 corks wide by 4 corks tall because that was a reasonable size for the shelf I had. The corks act as insulation so the hot glue will stay hot a bit longer than with other materials.

First, I hot glued the corks end to end, then used a small amount of hot glue down the side to join the rows together

The front wall is shorter and more narrow. I wanted the Faeries to have plenty of height for their wings once inside. I have no idea of their size! I also cut up the center of the door for the same reason.

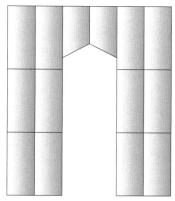

Cork pattern/front wall

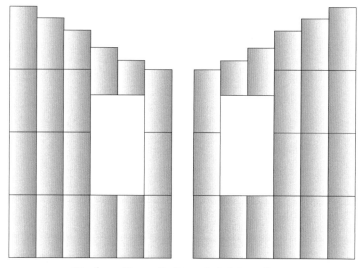

Cork pattern/left and right walls

The height of the corks can have some variation, as you will stuff any open spaces with moss. The front and sides make kind of a round corner, as neither side is exactly on the corner.

This pattern just happens to be what worked for the space I had, and seemed like a good size ... not too big, not too small, just right ... I hope!

AND FOR THE ROYAL FAERIE, HER OWN CASTLE

THE NEXT PROJECT I decided upon was to make a gift for a friend who happens to live at the beach. She works VERY hard at several jobs, so I decided she needed to come home to her own fantasy castle where she could play Alice in Wonderland, and imagine being inside it! Because she lives by the sea, the theme was the ocean, so perhaps she has a Mermaid living with her!

I went back to my watercolor paper for the walls, as it would never be outside. I found a beautiful big piece of crystal and built a strong enough base out of foam core board to support it. I made the roof 'removable' so my friend could lift it and look inside.

This is a pretty elaborate project, and not for the faint of heart. I certainly wouldn't start with this one, unless you are skilled at building these kinds of projects. On the inside, I made a little throne, and decorated it with some small jewelry crystal beads. I also made a fireplace to make it feel cozy. I made paintings on the wall of things my friend likes, and positioned the windows so that she could see through them to the inside of the house without removing the roof. For this project, I took a lot of photos throughout the process. I hope you find them helpful.

ASSEMBLY

You will need:
• heavy watercolor paper   • watercolor paint and brushes   • an X-acto® knife
• foam core board for the base support   • roofing material such as lavender
• a piece of wooden dowel for the flag   • a chunk of crystal (not necessary but a nice touch)
• a crystal for the top of the roof   • some kind of small tile for front porch
• clear matte acrylic paint   • hot glue and hot glue gun
• pearls and crystal beads for decoration
• iridescent white glitter for the floor inside (no moss for this queen!)

First, you will need to enlarge the pattern for the watercolor pieces provided at the end of this chapter, and cut out all the shapes. Cut the base out of foam core board just smaller than the water base shapes. Carefully paint all the pieces and the main walls, inside and out. Paint the flag, the roof (I just painted purple to match the lavender), the banner above the front door, the sea horses at the front door, and the throne. After everything is ,painted, coat with the clear acrylic inside and out.

For the outside walls, I first painted the brick pattern outline and after that had dried, I put a bluish wash over that. The pattern doesn't have to be bricks, in fact, can just be painted with vines if you prefer.

After the outside of the walls have dried, I turned them over and painted the inside. One wall painting is of a cat, as my friend loves her cat, and the other painting on the wall is of a mermaid ... appropriate! Also shown here are the water bases, the roof, the start of the banner over the door, and the throne has been folded and is just laying next to the fireplace.

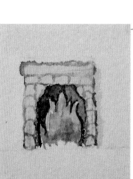

Sea horses to guard the front door. Close ups of the details inside. They are actually very small, and you should make the images be what ever entertains you! The throne is shaped but not yet mounted, and hasn't had the 'jewels' (small crystal beads) added yet.

Foam core base. Doesn't have to be perfect.

This is the banner before I folded it into final shape. You can choose to write whatever you want on your banner!

I gathered lavender from my yard, but any flower that will dry well will do, or can be purchased.

After hot gluing the seam of the roof to make a cone shape, start at the bottom edge and glue the flowers all around.

At the peak of the roof, hot glue on a quartz crystal.

For an added touch, glue pearls around the crystal.

The next step is to assemble the roof, as shown above. I used fresh lavender, but you can use anything, as long as it is natural. Sea shells would work if they were small enough, or even more pine cone scales.

Next, cut out little triangle pieces out of the part of the wall that will be glued to the base, to allow the wall to make a cylinder that is evenly round, and fold them inward. Assemble the throne with the crystal beads, and glue it to the inside wall. Then, glue it together on the side seam to make the cylindrical shape.

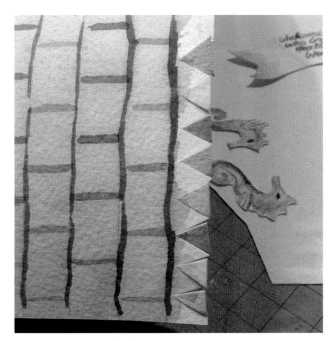

Cut little triangle shapes out of the bottom of the castle wall. You can just eyeball the size.

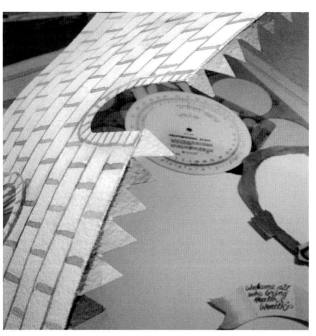

You can lightly score the bottom edge with the dull side of your X-acto where you are going to fold.

You can see that clipping around the bottom of the wall will make a round cylinder.

Glue the crystals to the arms of the throne, and glue the throne to the wall of the castle.

Next, add all the decorations to the outside of the castle, such as the sea horses and banner. You can put crystal beads above the door, and pearls around the windows.

Glue the two water pieces together, and then glue that to the foam core base.

Hot glue the decorations on the outside of the castle and then glue to the foam core base

Sprinkle iridescent glitter on the floor of the castle

Continue with the outside decorations, adding pearls around windows and base, crystal bead above the door, a square larger bead or tile for the 'drawbridge'. As you can see, the paintings on the inside walls are positioned to be viewed through the window openings.

For the final touches, hot glue the flag to the dowel, and glue the dowel to the castle wall at the seam. Then, hot glue your outside chunk of crystal next to it on the widest part of the water base. Make sure that you align the seam with the widest part of the water base, so the flag pole and crystal chunk are together there. The roof isn't permanently attached, so just set it on top. That allows for easy viewing of the inside.

Now, sit back, close your eyes, and just imagine who will come to visit this lovely and luxurious new home you have made!

28

Area of overlap to glue

Area where I placed painting of mermaid.

Area to attach throne.

Area where I painted fireplace.

You can leave the bottom folded area solid until after painting, then cut out V shapes. See photo instructions.

Squares are 1" x 1" so copy at 150% size to make them 1"
Solid lines are cut lines, dashed lines are score and fold lines

Area where I placed painting of cat.

Area of overlap to glue

29

30

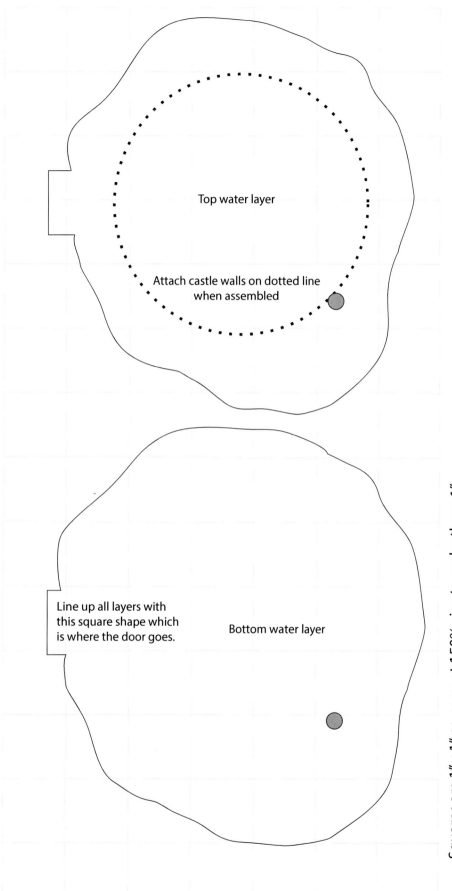

Top water layer

Attach castle walls on dotted line
when assembled

Line up all layers with
this square shape which
is where the door goes.

Bottom water layer

Squares are 1" x 1" so copy at 150% size to make them 1"
Solid lines are cut lines, dashed lines are score and fold lines

31

32

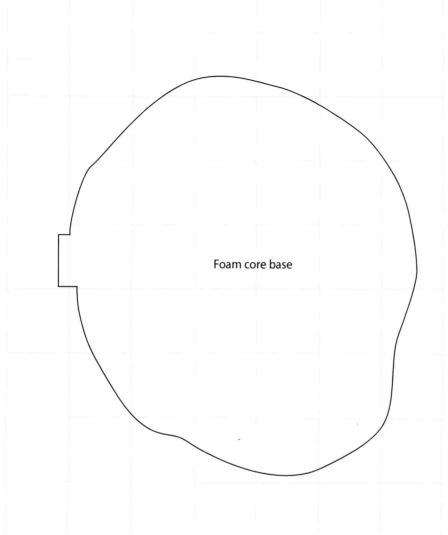

Foam core base

Squares are 1" x 1" so copy at 150% size to make them 1"
Solid lines are cut lines, dashed lines are score and fold lines

33

34

Throne

Banner above door

Seahorses beside door

Roof

Squares are 1" x 1" so copy at 100% size to make them 1"
Solid lines are cut lines, dashed lines are score and fold lines

35

36

A WEE HOUSE CHILDREN CAN MAKE

THE GRANDDAUGHTER OF A FRIEND OF MINE was visiting, and I thought it would be fun to have her make a Faerie House she could take home with her. I made a very simple shape and painted a sample for her to see. I didn't expect her young fingers to be able to paint the same detail that I had painted, but she had enough confidence to just charge forth and paint the bright and beautiful little house you see here, sitting in front of my more carefully painted one!

I had pre-cut out the watercolor paper, so all she had to do was paint away, using her imagination! After she left, and after the paint dried, I hot glued the house together for her, adding the usual crystal by the front door, of course. She was flying home on an airplane, so I provided a small but sturdy corrugated box for her to safely transport the house home with her. Once there, I suggested, if she wanted to, she could invite any Faeries that might be living around her to take up residence in her beautiful new home.

This is a perfect project for a child's party or a scout troop project. The fun is that they can be as carefree as they want with the color, but when the house is assembled by you afterwards, the physical structure makes the finished piece almost professional! I would make a sample one for them to see what they are aiming for, and if they get frustrated that they can't paint quite as precisely as your sample, encourage them to just be free, as the Faeries prefer freedom to preciseness! Another option is to supply stickers for them to use as decoration. Glitter paint in tubes could lend a bit of sparkle, too.

ASSEMBLY

You will need:
• heavy watercolor paper   • watercolor paint and brushes   • pencils for sketching
• a chunk of crystal (not necessary but a nice touch) • a piece of twine or yarn for hanging loop
• clear matte acrylic paint   • hot glue and hot glue gun • an X-acto® knife
• moss for the floor   • optional decorative stickers   • optional glitter paint

First, you will need to enlarge the pattern for the watercolor pieces provided at the end of this chapter, and cut out all the shapes. I made this house narrow and tall, assuming that no matter how small the Faerie, she would need room for her wings.

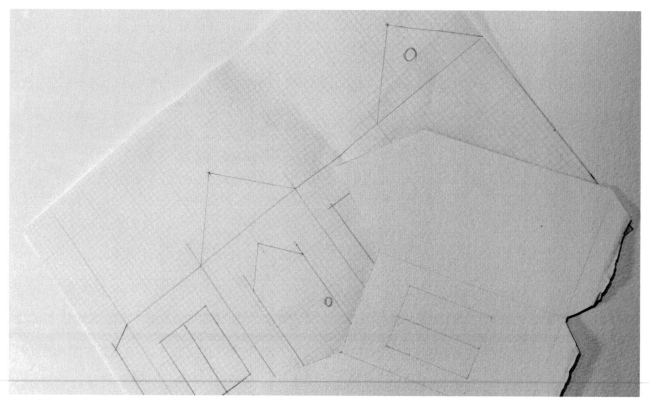

I drew the pattern on grid paper, but you can use your photocopy.

Cut and mark your sample first. As you can see, I made my pattern on grid paper, but just your enlarged copy on copy paper will do. Cut out the outside shape of the pattern, and tape to the watercolor paper. Cut out the water color paper with your X-acto knife. Then, to transfer all the lines to the water color paper, poke a little pin hole at each cor-

Note the small pin holes for transferring the drawing.

ner, then draw the pattern for the door and windows, and base fold line and corners in pencil on the watercolor paper, using the pin holes as guides. Don't cut them yet.

Next, paint your sample, inside and out, letting your imagination guide you as to what a real Faerie would like to see on her house! Paint the roof and base. Let the paper dry.

You can be as detailed or carefree as you like while painting your sample.

I chose to paint a fireplace inside, as it seemed inviting.

If you are not confident in your artistic skills, then you, too, can use stickers. Just paint the walls, doors, roof, base and window shutters flat color, and apply stickers when the paint is dry. Then, give all the pieces a good coat of clear matte acrylic paint, and let that dry.

Next, cut and fold all the doors, windows, corners and base folds. Open the shutters and door! Hot glue the side seam of the wall, hot glue the house to the base, then hot glue the roof to the top. If it is going to hang on the wall, hot glue the twine loop on the back, hot glue the crystal by the front door, and add the moss to the floor.

A crystal by the door ...

... and moss on the floor.

FOR THE CHILDREN'S PARTY

After you are happy with your sample, and have determined how many children will be participating (if more than one), cut and draw the pencil guidelines on their houses. It would be wise to make a couple of extra, in case an unexpected child shows up, or someone has a really distressful disaster!

Have plenty of brushes, paints and water ... and newspaper to work on. If you have really good quality watercolor brushes, unless the children are old enough to know how to use them, spare yourself the anxiety of watching them "scrub" the paper with your $30 brush! Provide them with decent quality but affordable brushes.

Encourage each child for their unique design. Ask them to imagine what THEIR Faerie would like to see outside and inside the house. Depending on their age, provide pencils for the children to sketch before they paint. If they ask you to paint a Faerie on the side of their house, feel free to contribute. This is a very interactive, creative process for both you and the children. If they aren't comfortable painting "things," have them just paint flat colors, let the color dry, and decorate with stickers. Then coat the houses and parts with the clear matte acrylic paint. Next, do the final window and door cutting and folding, and assemble the same way you did your sample. It isn't likely that they will take their Faerie House home with them that day (as you have to allow for drying time and time for you to do the final assembly.) Be sure to take plenty of photos during and after!

During the party, ask them to describe what their Faeries look like, what their Faeries like, how they act, what color they are, etc. Part of the act of making the houses is that they are really creating an imaginary space that someone just might come live in. Have them describe who that someone is!

There is a considerable amount of work to host a Faerie House-making party, but the rewards may surprise you, and this will likely be a special memory for the children, one they will one day want to repeat with THEIR children.

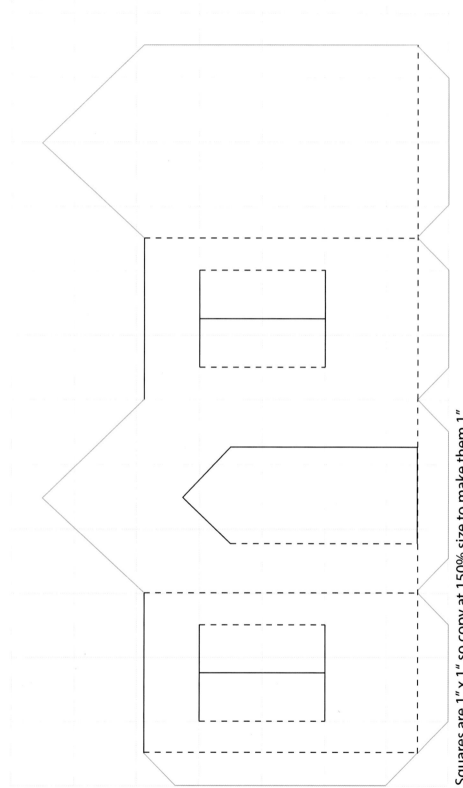

Squares are 1" x 1" so copy at 150% size to make them 1"
Solid lines are cut lines, dashed lines are score and fold lines

43

44

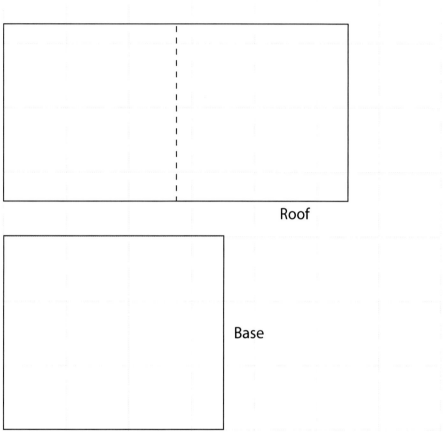

Roof

Base

Squares are 1" x 1" so copy at 150% size to make them 1"
Solid lines are cut lines, dashed lines are score and fold lines

45

46

THE POND STORY - A FAERIE HOUSE, FROG, BIRD AND A SNAKE

FOR SEVERAL YEARS, I worked with a group of concerned citizens opposing the building of the largest open pit gravel quarry less than one mile upwind of our home. The story lasted for 8 years of my life, so I won't go into detail about it here, other than to say that the Quarry did not get built and never will be. During that "battle," I struggled with the philosophy that you don't give energy to something you don't want, but rather give it to what you do want. So at one point, I decided that I would build a small fish pond with a curved "wall" directly facing the mountain endangered by the Quarry. I wanted to use a creative expression as an energy force to help keep the spirit of the mountain, and all that lived on it, intact.

The finished fish pond and wall of art.

The pond itself is very small, and has had an amazing amount of natural activity, considering that it is only 7.5 square feet of the total 14,810 square feet of our lot (.05%)!   The pond is cement, and the wall was built with concrete blocks and then covered with mosaic and rocks. I designed it so the water could come out of the top of the "waterfall," and I painted a tile with a mountain lion as if he is sitting on the edge of it.

The Quarry, if built, would have severed the only remaining wildlife corridor used by the mountain lions between the Coastal Mountains and the Palomar Mountains. That would have made the population of the mountain lions to the west too small to genetically survive in the long run. This was my sort of "art shield" directly facing the mountain, as if to say, "this mountain belongs to the mountain lions, not to a mega-quarry."

I also painted a tile with a Kestrel Falcon, as when we first moved here, they would nest in our roof every year. When their young would fledge, they would disappear until the next year. The quarry would have filled the air with silica, making life difficult for all of nature, birds included.

On the side of the wall, I painted tiles with this statement:

Tiles on the side of the wall.

God granted a
deed to the animals
for a place in the sky,
on the land,
and in the water.
Man's job is to
recognize and honor
that deed so that
he need never
walk here alone.

I painted an image of a frog on the tile, so I guess that was also an invitation for one to come live with us! There is a great deal of distance between the pond and any other body of water, so I was quite surprised one day, despite my painted invitation, to find one living in the pond. I have no idea how it got there ... must have hopped a very long way across dry ground ... but he found us, and made the pond his home.

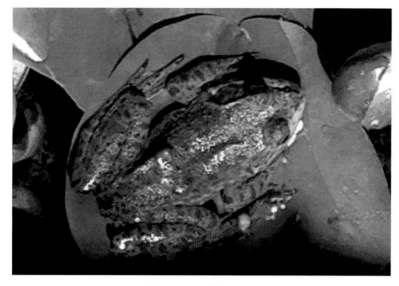

Our sweet froggie.

I decided that I would build a pond Faerie House to invite a Faerie to come and be friends with the frog. I planned on it being in a fern pot near the pond, and planned to make a little floating pier so she could sit on it and talk to the frog. This little house had to be sturdy, as I have to keep the fern watered every few days.

I started with a milk carton, and built the house around it. All those directions will follow, but now I must tell you the rest of the pond story.

I keep the pond filled with simple gold fish. It is under an arbor, so the fish there are somewhat protected from predatory birds. One day, in the summer of 2015, I looked out the window, and there was a Great Blue Heron standing by the pond! What a sight! With neck extended, it was about 3' tall and not afraid of us or our noisy dogs. The heron spent

This giant magical bird was not the least bit afraid of us, taking up residence on the Jacuzzi shade!

every day with us for more than a week. It took up residence, and would be there first thing in the morning. I'm not sure if it slept in the yard, but I wouldn't be surprised.

Well, you can guess the sad ending to the never-to-be-written Faerie and Frog story. Before I had built the pond Faerie House, all the fish and the frog disappeared, obviously into the belly of the big blue bird. So, instead of a fantasy story I was creating in my imagination, I had a real life nature story acting out on the stage that was my pond. Ah, such is life.

I have to say that the visit by the heron was a very magical experience. The fish are called "feeder fish," as people buy them to feed to their turtles. They had a much longer life than expected, living in our pond. I do regret the loss of the frog. His appearance was just as magical as the visits by the heron. I am so grateful for the awesome display of nature they presented to us.

But there is even more to this pond story that summer. We live right on the edge of a Southern California nature area. Between our yard and the open hillsides, there is a dry

water release valve

faucet on wall

de-chlorinator

can you see the snake?

The water barrel behind the art wall ... and the barely visible rattlesnake.

creek bed and a golf course. There are coyotes that hunt up and down the creek, and we have had in our yard skunks, a raccoon, possums, and snakes.

Because the water evaporates quickly in our dry climate, I have a water barrel behind the pond wall that I fill with water to put in dechlorinator before flowing the water into the pond. Fish don't like chlorine. One day, I stood with my feet right next to the barrel to close the barrel valve, filled it with water, put in the dechlorinator, and then reached down again and opened the valve to let the water flow into the pond. Right after that, I had the hose turned on, and backed up with it to start watering plants. I just happened to look back, and see that there was a large rattlesnake coiled up under the water barrel, right where I had been standing ...

within inches of the snake! I see why they have those markings, as the rattlesnake blended right into the leaves.

I screamed, we called Animal Control, and in about 45 minutes they arrived. The snake didn't move that whole time, but was very agitated when Animal Control came after it with the snake stick.

I tell you this story because it is part of the nature drama that unfolded around our little pond that summer. We have a pool and Jacuzzi, but that doesn't attract life. This little pond does. The miracle of this part of the story is that the rattlesnake did not bite me.

A friend of mine had been bitten in her yard a few months before, and she was in the hospital for several days, even though she arrived at the hospital within 20 minutes of being bitten.

I previously created a deck of message cards called Voice of the Soul (www.voiceofsoul. org,) and about the time of my rattlesnake incident, my husband drew the "Sunrise" card; so, I painted this little reminder of that day … of among other things, to be grateful for, the rattlesnake not biting me.

So after all the adventure, I did build the pond Faerie House, and the instructions are on the following pages. After I put the house next to the pond, one day I noticed that there was a kind of moss growing next to the pond that I had never seen before. Was that a sign someone had move into the house? I like to think so!

I share this little adventure story with you to encourage you to be open to your own adventures in your yard or house, or in the park nearby. There is much to be gained personally by reaching out to the world of nature. We are, after all, part of it and it, is part of us. For too many centuries, we have exercised our will to control nature. Perhaps it is time to instead exercise our creativity to embrace it.

The Pond Faerie House tucked away near the pond.

Never before seen moss that grew after the Faerie House was installed.

ASSEMBLY

You will need:
• a large milk carton • a collection of twigs • a ruler and marker • grout
• a large pine cone • garden clippers • a crystal for the top • optional dry grass for one side
• hot glue and hot glue gun • glass tiles for windows • copper foil for roof
• moss for the floor • rocks for base • optional glitter paint or gold foil for inside
• glue for glitter • glass beads for "tree" • palette knife • wide flat brush

Take your milk carton, and mark where you want the door, windows and roofline. I used a glass tile at the top of the front above the door, and one on the side for a window. These are not essential, but since this will be outdoors, and I believe the Faeries would like some light inside their home, it seems worth the effort to find the glass tiles.

 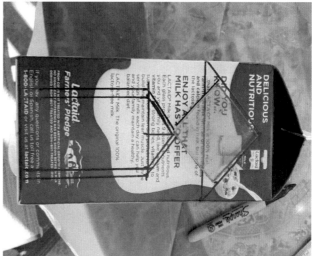

Planning out all sides of the house.

Cut out the door and window shapes, but not the roofline yet. Just cut off the top of the carton square. You need to keep the carton stable while you work on the bottom. Turn over and hot glue rocks to the bottom of the carton. Because it will be outside, and likely near plants you will be watering, you don't want the base of the carton to get wet, so the rocks lift it up safely off the ground. Put a generous amount of grout between the rocks. I used white grout on the bottom, and brown grout on the sides, but you can use the same grout for both bottom and sides.

Cut door and window but not roofline just yet.   *Rocks on bottom will keep the base dry.*

Next, you will break or cut all your twigs to fit the sides. You might want to use garden clippers to do this. You can start gluing the bottom twigs before you turn it right side up. Once upright, cut the roofline to its final shape. You can cut the twigs to shape as you glue them, as you won't know how much space each one will take.

Hot glue the glass tiles (windows) in place, and "frame" the side window with some twigs.

On one side of the house, I just hot glued a dried grass material, as I ran out of twigs, and this was an easy solution. The grass material was purchased at Michael's.

Next, you will mix up your grout to a semi-liquid consistency. Keep adding water and the grout powder back and forth, blending until you get it to a workable consistency. Too dry, and it won't fill in the cracks – too wet, and it will flow right out.

House ready for grouting.

Apply a ridge of grout with your fingers to support and stabilize the windows.

Trial and error mixing grout to correct consistency.

Using your fingers, push some of the grout up to the glass tile windows to support them. Do this on all sides of the side window and on the bottom of the window on the front of the house.

Next comes the fun, messy part! Once you start this process, you can't stop until you are finished, as you don't want the grout to dry before you have brushed it away from the surface of the twigs. That has to be done when the grout is wet.

Using a palette knife, apply a generous amount of the grout to the twig covered areas, one side at a time.

Applying the grout with a palette knife.

Before you move on to the next side, use a wide paint brush, dipped in water, and brush away the excess grout to reveal the twigs, but leaving the grout between near the surface.

When you are satisfied with each side, move on to the next side, finishing with the grass side if you decided to make one side grass.

"Washing" away the excess grout with a wet brush, continually dipped in water.

Allow the little house at least overnight to dry and set. Then you can move on to decorating the inside walls. I coated the walls with glue, then scattered on some iridescent flakes and some gold flakes that I had. This should please any Faerie that would choose to live here.

Grout applied to the grass side of the house before the excess is brushed away.

Sparkle and gold flakes applied to the inside walls.

Gluing on of the copper roof.

Next you will create the roof. Measure and cut the copper foil to overhang the sides, front and back of the house. Cut, fold in half and hot glue to the house.

Create the shingles for the roof by clipping off the scales of your pine cone. They don't just "fall" off easily so, I used my garden clippers to cut them off. Once they have all been removed from the pine cone, attach them to the roof starting at the bottom row. I originally used hot glue, but in time they popped off, so I recommend using Gorilla Glue®, keeping in mind that the glue expands as it sets. (See example in the "Before you Begin" section at the front of the book.)

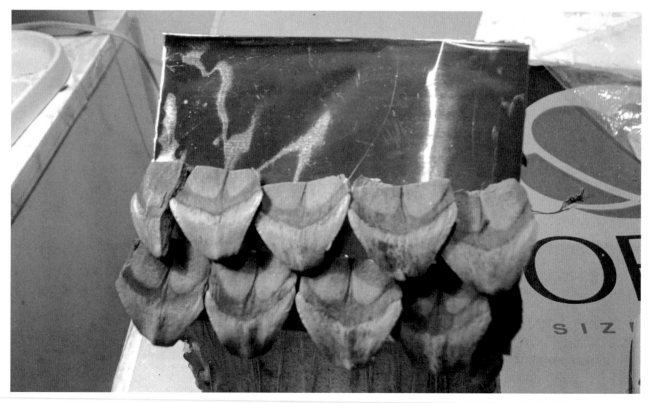

Applying the shingles on the roof, starting with the bottom row.

Cut a narrow strip of the copper foil the depth of the roof, and fold in half for the center top of the roof.

You can use the top of the pine cone to create a topper for the front of the roof. I hot glued a crystal in the middle to get it ready to attach. I then attached it with hot glue to the folded copper foil strip and let it stabilize. Next I hot glued that strip, complete with topper, to the roof top.

Detail of "crown" for front of roof. The copper spine with the detail attached to roofline.

For a final and optional touch, I used the pine cone without its scales to make a "tree" to sit next to the house. I simply hot glued a cross of twigs to the bottom for a base, and then hot glued the small glass balls to add some decoration. Again, in time, these popped out, so using Gorilla Glue from the beginning might be a better idea. Put some moss on the floor for "comfort."

You are now ready to install your house and tree somewhere outside. As I have said, in my case, it was near my small fish pond. Walk around your yard and see if you can "feel" the right space. Look for an area where plants seem to be doing well as evidence someone might already be there!

Base stand of the tree and the completed, decorated tree.

This is really an opportunity for you, as a adult, to allow yourself the child-like optimism that it is possible to support the "unseen" spirits of nature. There can be no harm in this, and it has great potential for opening a new "house" in your heart for all things small and delicate.

The completed house and yard, ready to welcome a new resident!

MUSHROOMS, GOURDS, AND A FAERIE GARDEN

WHY WOULD A WHOLE CROP OF MUSHROOMS suddenly sprout in my yard, where they had never been before? I wasn't at all sure, but decided that there must be a Mushroom Faerie living there, so I had to make it a Faerie Home. It came together quickly and easily, so I felt I had really 'heard' Mother Nature speaking.

That area of our yard had been somewhat neglected, and there was a broken wheelbarrow just taking up space, so I cut off the broken front wheel and tilted the wheelbarrow to make the garden home. I decided I would to learn how to make a sturdy Faerie House using a dried gourd, so I found a gourd supplier on the Internet and ordered a nice plump round one. After I made this home, mushrooms started popping up all around the yard, despite the fact that the weather had turned cold. Within a couple of weeks, the most amazing tall mushroom with a lace skirt sprouted just a few feet from the new Mushroom Faerie's home! It only lasted a day, so I was very glad to have captured it in my camera!

The surprise 'lace skirted' mushroom that sprouted near the Mushroom Faerie House, lasting only one day.

It turns out that these homes made from gourds are the easiest to make and they do hold up well outdoors (so far anyway). I found a vendor at my local farmers market who sells dried gourds, so I pick up a few every week. They are also easy to get on the Internet. I decorate each house with a crystal and those I purchase from another fellow at my the farmers market, They, too, are easy to acquire on the Internet. You can get as creative as you like with these, or keep them simple, too. Just think of what the Faerie would like. I make the doors tall and narrow, and put some kind of window in each house. There is no actual door to close, but even so, I believe the gourd provides shelter for the Faeries. I cut up an old sweater with moth holes in it for the floor to make it soft. I don't really know what Faeries need beyond that ... just shelter from the wind and the rain and the sun, and an acknowledgment that they are welcome!

After I made the first gourd home, I decided I would make one for our two great-nieces and one for our two great-nephews. The gourds I purchased from the farmers market had long, arched stems so they look a bit like ducks. I found a little statue of a Faerie to give the girls, and a little Elf for the boys. I used small glass tiles for the windows, one on each side, held in place with the clay. I think the Faeries appreciate even a small window.

Faerie and Elf houses made for the children in our family.

I always put a small crystal somewhere near the door, in this case in the center of the leaf. I found two nice pieces of polished stone for the doorsteps. After I made the original Mushroom Faerie House, I was concerned about rain getting in the front door, so for these I made a leaf out of the clay to keep most of the rain water out. The gourds are a bit wobbly, so I made a base for them. I also decided to put a couple of coats of varnish on these two so they would hold up better outside.

As I write this, the great-nieces have finished their garden. Because they live close by, we were able to provide the box, dirt, tiles and plants for them. We also made a tiny table and bench from some stones we found in the yard. The great-nephews live in a stormy part of the country, so they can't make their garden until the Spring. Since siblings have different opinions over such decisions as to where to plant each plant, it is a good teaching opportunity to explain that if they are arguing while making the garden, they will attract a grumpy Faerie to live there, so they should make an effort to cooperate with each other.

ASSEMBLY

You will need:
• a dried gourd   • DAS Air Hardening Modeling Clay, either white or clay colored
• clay molding tools • a dremel tool • a pencil • silicone seal
• Plaster of Paris if you want for the floor • some soft material for the carpet
• one or two small quartz crystals   • an optional stone for the doorstep
• glass tiles for windows   • wax paper and a rolling pin   • glue   • optional varnish

Decide where your gourd Faerie House will be located, then design and plant the garden. It can be in a container or in an small area of your yard. You can do this before or after you make your Faerie House, as long as you have the gourd to know how much space to allow for it. Find a local nursery that has a selection of miniature plants that will STAY small. Many nurseries now offer Faerie Garden workshops, providing the container, plants and guidance. If you do that, be sure to bring your gourd with you to the class. Careful planning

I located the garden near the mushrooms and planted the faerie garden. With Bentley supervising, I placed the untouched gourd to decide which side should have the front door.

of the garden is as important as making the house itself. For this Mushroom Faerie garden, I used an old wheelbarrow, cut off the front wheel and drilled holes in the bottom of the wheelbarrow for drainage. Be sure to place a layer of stones or tiles in your garden to set the Faerie House on.

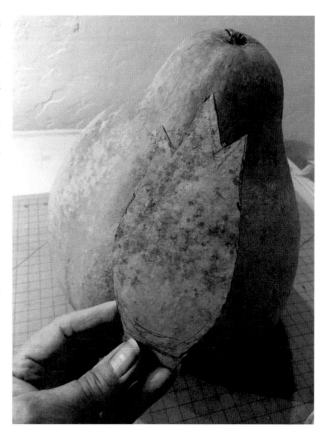

To make the house, draw your door and window shapes on the gourd. The door can be drawn freehand, but for the window(s), you should trace around the clear material you are going to use. For this one, I found a flat 'sheet' of quartz crystal for the window, but you can use any kind of glass tile.

With great care not to cut yourself, use a small rotary blade with your dremel tool to cut out the shapes. You will be covering the edges with clay so they don't have to be perfect. I use the Dremel® 199 High Speed Cutter.

Roll out a long piece of clay and press it onto the edges of the window opening. Then press the window into place and 'mold' the clay onto the edges inside and out by reaching through the door opening. Be creative and 'organic' with this molding. Don't think of it as a perfectly squared off human window, think of it as shapes that would naturally occur and be pleasing to a creature of nature, as if it 'grew' that way!

The clay will air dry in 24 hours, and to assure a watertight seal, after the clay was dry, I applied silicone seal around the edges of the crystal window.

Next, use the same method of rolling out a long piece of clay and pressing it against the edges of the door. I made the center of the door tall and pointy to accommodate the wings of the Faerie. I placed two quartz crystals above the door – a large one on the left, and a small one on the right. After the clay dries, if the crystals aren't secure, be sure to glue them in place. You can use any glue that will tolerate freezing if it is to be outside in 32 degree or below temperatures.

Now you are ready to make the decorative leaves and stem for the top. Flatten out

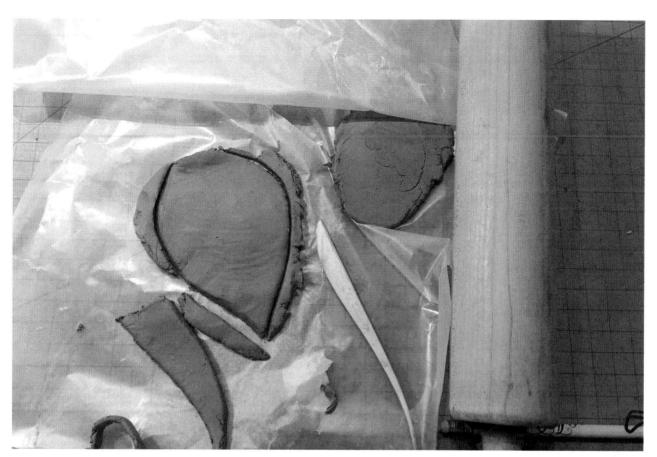

some clay and place between two pieces of wax paper. Use your rolling pin to flatten the clay evenly. Cut out your leaf shapes, (in this case, I made three), add veins, and shape and drape them over the top of the gourd. Roll a very long piece of clay to a pointed end and make the stem shape at the top as shown.

After all the clay has dried (in about a day), clean up the edges of the clay with water and then glue all the pieces securely in place.

If it is going to be outside, I would give the gourd a couple of coats of varnish. I did not with this one, and it seems to be holding up just fine. The clay absorbs a slight amount of rainwater, but it holds its shape.

Two different ways to stabilize the round bottomed gourd house. In the left photo, mix some Plaster of Paris and fill the bottom to add weight. In the right photo, make a base of clay and, when dry, glue it to the gourd.

The door was a bit high off the ground, so I made some flat pieces of clay and stacked them up to make a front step.

Because the gourds are round on the bottom, there are a couple of things you can do to stabilize them. On the first one, I made up a small batch of Plaster of Paris and put it on the inside to make a floor and to give it enough weight to stabilize it. On the next gourd, I made a "base" of clay and glued it onto the bottom when the clay was dry. Either way seems to work just fine.

Find a nice soft material for the 'carpet,' such as an old sweater or moss, and line the bottom of the gourd.

When placing the house in the garden, make a base for it of flat rocks or tiles. This will keep the gourd from sitting directly on the dirt and moisture, and keep it whole for a longer period of time. You can make the garden in a container, or build it directly in your yard around the Faerie House with no container at all. Making these Faerie Houses out of gourds is an opportunity to be creative and to let Nature know that you welcome Her into your house or garden! Observe how well the plants do when being attended to by your befriended Faerie!

I might even suggest that you keep a journal about what you observe ... and that could one day even turn into your own Faerie Tale! Or, just keep it simple and enjoy the experience for just that – the experience. Have fun!

72

IN CONCLUSION ...

I AM SO PLEASED I to share with you my personal journey with Faerie Houses. When I first acknowledged how well the orchids did in my kitchen window, and, on a whim, decided to built my first Faerie House, I had no idea where this was going to take me.

If something is holding your curiosity, perhaps you should travel along with it and see where it takes you. It doesn't have to be Faerie Houses. It could be making inspirational jewelry, making quilts that are art, planting an inviting garden, learning to sing again, learning to play an instrument you did have time for in another part of your life, or forming a book club ... shall I go on?

This book is really written for adults as these Faerie Houses are, other then the two designed for children, too complex for children to make. If you do decide to build one, you can influence the children around you to keep their optimism open longer. Puppies and children have such joyful and playful optimism. Any effort to value that may reward you in surprising way.

Re-opening your own optimism is a great a gift you can give yourself, too. So what is your story? Now is the time to let it unfold. Now is the time, you are the person ... let the happiness begin!

74

75

76